Michael Jordan. People in every country know that name. They know his face. They know his number: 23. He is tall and strong. He has a lot of money. He is very famous. And he can fly!

Michael Jordan is a basketball player. He played for thirteen years for the Chicago Bulls.* Many people understand basketball. A lot of people love basketball. But Michael Jordan *lives* basketball. Every game is important to him. But where did he come from? How did he win six NBA† championships? When did he start to fly?

Early Days

Michael's story starts on February 17, 1963, in Brooklyn, New York. The family moves to Wilmington, North Carolina later in 1963. Michael is the son of Deloris and James Jordan. He comes from a happy home with a lot of love. One old friend says, "The Jordans' door was always open. Mr. and Mrs. Jordan talked to us and listened to us. There was always a basketball game in the back yard."

Young Michael's best friend is his brother, Larry. Larry teaches his little brother a lot of things about basketball. Mr. Jordan builds a big basketball court for

---

* Chicago Bulls, Houston Rockets, Portland Trailblazers, Los Angeles Lakers, Washington Wizards: NBA basketball teams.
† NBA: the best basketball teams in the US play for the NBA.

his sons and their friends. This is Michael's first basketball school.

Today, Michael says, "We played basketball games every day. On Saturdays, we were on our court all day. Rain? No problem. We played basketball."

For a long time, Larry is the best basketball player in the Jordan family. Baseball is Michael's game. He is strong and quick. He always wants to win.

The Jordan children have jobs at home, but Michael doesn't like working. His brothers and sisters have money for things. Michael doesn't have any money because he doesn't work. The only jobs in his life are baseball and basketball.

Basketball at School

From twelve to fifteen years old Michael plays baseball, basketball, and football at school. He is short for a basketball player: he is only 1.75 meters (5'9"). Mr. and Mrs. Jordan are under 1.75 meters. Michael isn't going to be very tall.

In 1978, Michael starts his three years at Laney High School. His teachers say now, "Michael was a good student. He was quiet, but he had a lot of friends."

Michael starts basketball at Laney on the "A" team. Larry is on the "A" team, too. He has number 45. Michael asks for number 23 because $45 \div 2 = 22\frac{1}{2}$. But Michael doesn't stay on the "A" team. The coach moves him to the "B" team.

"Michael was a good student."

Michael is angry. He wants to be on the best team. He plays basketball every morning, afternoon, and evening. Sometimes, he doesn't go to school. His father talks to him. Basketball is important, but school is important, too. Michael goes back to school.

It is the summer of 1979. Mr. Jordan remembers, "Michael wanted to be tall. He wanted to be on the 'A' team. Suddenly he was 1.91 meters (6'3") tall." In September, Michael plays on the "A" team. He is the star of basketball at Laney.

The "A" team games start at seven-thirty in the evening. Before five o'clock, the people of Wilmington are waiting at the court. They want to see Michael. Laney wins its first championship that year.

College Life

Now Michael thinks about basketball after Laney. A lot of colleges want him. Michael likes the University of North Carolina (UNC) in Chapel Hill. He likes the basketball coach, Dean Smith. Michael goes to UNC in September, 1981, with his sister Roslyn. She is a very good student, and she starts college early.

Dean Smith teaches Michael a lot of things about basketball. "Remember, every player on the team is important," he says. Michael works on his game. He is on the first team in his first year at UNC.

Michael is the best new player in college basketball in 1981–2. The UNC team, the Tar Heels, get to the 1982 college basketball championships. They are going to play the Georgetown Hoyas.

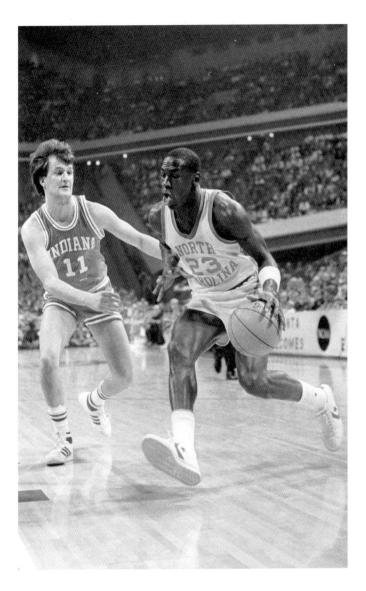

Michael is the best new player in college basketball.

There are 61,000 people in New Orleans for the big game. It is Tar Heels 61, Hoyas 62. There is only a little time in the game now. Dean Smith says to his players, "Get the ball to Michael." Michael has the ball. The Hoyas run at him. But Michael doesn't look at the players. He looks at the basket. He takes a long shot. The ball is in the basket. UNC wins its first college championship.

The story of "the shot" is in the newspapers and on TV. Michael is famous. His photo and "the shot" are on the Chapel Hill telephone book in 1982.

"The shot"

The NBA, 1984–93

Every year, the teams in the NBA look for good new players. After three important and happy years at UNC, Michael Jordan thinks about the NBA. But Deloris Jordan says to her son, "Finish your four years at UNC. It's very important."

Michael says, "I'm going to go to the NBA. But I'm going to finish my college work, too." (Michael finishes his work at UNC in 1986. His mother is very happy!)

In June of 1984, the NBA teams are looking for tall players. Michael is 1.98 meters (6'6"). He isn't very tall for the NBA. The Houston Rockets take Hakeem Olajuwon (2.08 meters; 6'10"). The Portland Trailblazers take Sam Bowie (2.16 meters; 7'1"). Then, at number three, Jordan hears his name. The Chicago Bulls want him.

The Bulls aren't a good team in 1984. They win only twenty-seven of eighty-two games. But they give Michael $6,000,000 for seven years.

The Bulls always say to their players, "You play for *us* now. No basketball on your vacations. This is your job." But Michael wants to play with his friends and with Larry. The Bulls want Michael. They say, "OK, Michael, you can play for us. And you can play for 'love of the game,' too."

In July of 1984, Michael catches an airplane to Los Angeles. He is on the 1984 US Olympic★ basketball

★ Olympic Games: every four years, many countries send teams to these games.

7

team. The best college players in the country are on the team. They win their games and the Olympic award for basketball. Michael gives his award to his mother. (He plays again, and wins, in the 1992 Olympic Games.)

After the 1984 Olympic Games, Michael starts his job with the Bulls. In the NBA, he can be a big star on the basketball court.

Nike makes shoes for basketball players. People from Nike say, "This new star can fly. He's going to be very famous." Nike makes a shoe for Michael. Its name is "Air Jordan." Now Michael plays and people say, "Can he fly? Or is it the shoes?"

People buy a lot of "Air Jordan" shoes. In two years, Nike makes $130,000,000 from them. Michael makes a lot of money from them, too.

Michael loves the NBA. His game is strong. People like watching him. But life away from the basketball court is often difficult. People always want to talk to him. Michael can't walk down the street. He can't go to a store or to a movie. People want to be his friend.

In 1985, Michael meets Juanita Vanoy. She is smart and beautiful and interesting. But she doesn't know about basketball. She likes Michael because he is a good person. They want the same things in life.

From 1984 to 1987, Michael wins a lot of awards in the NBA. But he wants to win the NBA championship. The newspapers ask, "Is Jordan a team player? Can the Bulls win the championship?"

From 1987 to 1990, the Bulls get some new players and a new coach, Phil Jackson. The Bulls start to build a championship team.

In the NBA, Michael can be a big star.

In December 1988, there is a very happy story in the newspapers. Michael and Juanita have their first son. His name is Jeffrey.

The 1990–91 Bulls are very good. They win sixty-one of eighty-two games. The Bulls and the Los Angeles Lakers are in the championship games. The Bulls win the championship in five games. Michael says, "We're a strong team. After seven years, we did it!"

Now no team can stop the Bulls. They win the championship in 1992 and in 1993. The newspapers say, "Michael Jordan is the best. He can win every game."

Michael has many awards and three championships in three years. He and Juanita now have two sons, Jeffrey and Marcus, and one daughter, Jasmine. After the championships in 1993, Michael goes home with his family. He is strong and happy.

A New Baseball Star?

Things are good for the Jordan family in the summer of 1993. But then, one day, Michael's father visits some friends. That evening, he doesn't come home. The police find him in a river. Two eighteen–year-old boys killed him for his car and his money.

Michael loved his father very much, and he can't understand this. Why did these boys kill a good man?

On October 6, 1993, Michael and Juanita are on TV. Michael says, "Life is very short. I want to have time with my family." Michael retires from basketball. The Bulls retire his number, 23.

Michael and Juanita

Early in 1994, Michael starts a new job in baseball. Michael and a lot of young players try for a place on the Chicago White Sox baseball team. Michael can run well. He can catch well. But he can't hit a baseball very well. The newspapers say, "Mike, please! Come back to basketball!"

But Michael likes playing baseball. In baseball he isn't a star. Michael's number is 45, Larry's old number. But in August, 1994, there are problems in baseball about money. The players stop the games. They don't play for a long time. Michael is thirty-one years old. He can't wait for baseball.

Michael starts a new job in baseball.

The NBA, 1995–8

On March 8, 1995, the Chicago Bulls' office gives a story to the newspapers. It is a short story from Michael Jordan. It says, "I'm back." Chicago is a very happy town that night.

Michael is happy with the Bulls again and with his old friends and his coach, Phil Jackson. The team works well and starts to win again.

Michael is number 45 in the championship games. The Bulls aren't doing very well. Some players say, "Number 45 is OK. But number 23 was a star." This makes Michael angry. He goes back to number 23. Now the players remember, "He's back!"

The Bulls don't win the championship in 1995. In the summer, Michael has some time. He makes a movie: "Space Jam." Children love it. It makes a lot of money.

The Bulls start 1995–6 with a new player, Dennis Rodman, and some old players, Scottie Pippen and Michael Jordan. The Bulls are the best team in the NBA again. And Michael Jordan is their star.

The Bulls win the NBA championship in 1996, 1997, and 1998. Michael Jordan has six NBA championship awards. And he has basketball awards in every room in his house.

But there are always problems in life. The Chicago Bulls' office wants a new coach. But Michael Jordan likes playing for Phil Jackson.

The NBA players are unhappy about their money, too. They start the games late in 1998.

Michael can fly!

Then Michael is on TV again. He retires from basketball on January 13, 1999.

Michael has a lot of money from his life in basketball. In 2000, he buys an NBA team, the Washington Wizards. They aren't a good team. Michael starts to play again. He plays for his team, and he plays some strong games. The Washington Wizards can fly! But Michael sometimes has problems with his legs. Is he going to retire—again?

In 2003, Michael Jordan is forty years old. He doesn't play often now but he loves the game. Basketball is Michael's life.

ACTIVITIES

Pages 1–6

Before you read

1 What do you know about Michael Jordan? Why is he famous?

2 Look at the Word List at the back of the book.
    a What are these words in your language?
    b Talk about football, basketball, or baseball with these words:

    award   ball   championship   coach   star   team   win

    Would you like the life of a famous player? Why (not)?

While you read

3 Write the names of these people, places, and things.
    a Michael's team for thirteen years   ....
    b Michael's first home town   ....
    c Michael's second home town   ....
    d Michael's mother and   .... and
       father   ....
    e Michael's brother   ....
    f Michael's high school   ....
    g Michael's number   ....
    h Michael's college   ....
    i Michael's college coach   ....
    j the year of "the shot"   ....

After you read

4 Work with a friend. It is 1979.
    Student A: You are Michael Jordan. Talk to your father or mother about your life. What do you want to do now?
    Student B: You are James or Deloris Jordan. Talk to your son, Michael, about his life. What is important? What is not important?

Pages 7–15

Before you read

5 After the 1982 college basketball championships, Michael is famous. What is he going to do now? Talk about it.

While you read

6 Circle the right answer.

a Michael Jordan *finishes / doesn't finish* his college work.

b The Chicago Bulls *don't win / win* the NBA championship in 1984.

c The US Olympic basketball team wins in *1982 and 1986 / 1984 and 1992*.

d "Air Jordan" is *a basketball team / a shoe.*

e Juanita Vanoy *knows / doesn't know* about basketball.

f Michael and Juanita Jordan have *one son and two daughters / two sons and one daughter*.

g Two boys kill Michael's *father / mother* in 1993.

h In 1994, Michael can *hit / catch* a baseball very well.

i Chicago is a *happy / unhappy* town on March 8, 1995.

j In the 1990s, the Chicago Bulls win *three / six* NBA championships.

k Michael Jordan is *the writer / the star* of the movie "Space Jam".

l From 2000 to 2003, Michael Jordan plays for *the Chicago Bulls / the Washington Wizards*.

After you read

7 Phil Jackson is talking to five new players on his team. Write his words.

8 You work for a newspaper. You are going to meet Michael Jordan. Write ten questions for him.

WORD LIST *with example sentences*

award (n) The school gives *awards* every year to good students.

ball (n) Catch the *ball*—don't hit it!

baseball (n) We like to watch football and *baseball*.

basket(ball) (n) In a game of *basketball*, you put the ball in the *basket*.

best (adj) He is the *best* student in the school.

championship (n) The first games of the *championship* are in September.

coach (n) He isn't one of the players. He is their *coach*.

college (n) My family lives in Mississippi, but I go to *college* in Virginia.

court (n) Why are there only nine players on the *court*?

fly (v) I can drive to Chicago and then *fly* to Los Angeles.

high school (n) My sister didn't finish *high school*. She works in a store.

kill (v) She *killed* her father with a knife.

life (n) I don't remember my *life* in Alaska because I was very young then.

meter (n) Their new kitchen is ten *meters* long!

retire (v) She doesn't work. She *retired* from her job this year.

shot (n) Take a *shot*. Can you hit the tree?

star (n) George Clooney is a movie *star*.

team (n) David Beckham was in the England *team* for years.

university (n) He went to Harvard *University* and then worked for his father.

win (v) I watch the Dallas Mavericks because they *win* a lot of games.

Pearson Education Limited
Edinburgh Gate, Harlow,
Essex CM20 2JE, England
and Associated Companies throughout the world.

ISBN: 978-1-4058-8151-7

First published by Penguin Books 2001
This edition first published 2008

5

Typeset by Graphicraft Ltd, Hong Kong
Set in 12/14pt Bembo
Printed in China
SWTC/05

Published by Pearson Education Ltd

Acknowledgements:
Yearbook Archives: p. 3; Corbis: pp. 5, 6, and 11;
All Sport USA: pp. 9 and 14; Rex Features: p. 12

Every effort has been made to trace the copyright holders and we apologise in advance
for any unintentional omissions. We would be pleased to insert the appropriate
acknowledgement in any subsequent edition of this publication.

For a complete list of the titles available in the Pearson English Readers series, please visit
www.pearsonenglishreaders.com. Alternatively, write to your local Pearson Education
office or to Pearson English Readers Marketing Department, Pearson Education,
Edinburgh Gate, Harlow, Essex CM20 2JE, England.